Edwin Beard

Life Lines

Edwin Beard

Life Lines

ISBN/EAN: 9783337054403

Printed in Europe, USA, Canada, Australia, Japan

Cover: Foto ©ninafisch / pixelio.de

More available books at **www.hansebooks.com**

Life Lines.
BEARD.

ILLUSTRATED.

1898
Iroquois County Times Print,
WATSEKA ILL.

COPYRIGHT.

Entered according to act of Congress, in the year 1898,

By EDWIN BEARD,

In the Office of the Librarian of Congress, at Washington, D. C.

ALL RIGHTS RESERVED.

Illustrations by Geo. H. Benedict & Co.,
CHICAGO.

PREFACE.

IN placing this volume before the public the author is not in quest of fame. Had such been the motive, better judgment might have suggested the traveling of some other road to find it. Our chief desire has been to collate and preserve such of the stanzas written during a brief but busy career that would best illustrate the nobler impulses and thoughts of life. Some of the contents of the succeeding pages, friends have seen proper to denominate as "Poems." They may be mistaken. If conscientious in their judgment they will not be held accountable for damages. The Author.

DEDICATION.

THIS volume is dedicated to a Devoted Wife, whose loving presence has prompted the impulse and inspiration of many of its stanzas, and whose gentle importunities have been an impelling power in the search for plans that have made its publication possible under adverse circumstances and conditions which, otherwise, might not have been overcome. —E. B.

CONTENTS.

Portrait of Author,	Frontispiece
Preface,	7
Dedication,	8
Buds and Blossoms, (Illustrated)	13
Seven Years,	15
A Mother's Love,	16-17
Now,	18
The Child,	19-20-21
The Ship of Life,	22-23
Forgetfulness of Fate,	24
Keep the Main-Traveled Road,	25
The Sun-Flower, (Illustrated)	26
A Thanksgiving Plea for the Poor,	27
Life's Seasons—	
Spring, (Illustrated)	28
Summer, (Illustrated)	29
Autumn, (Illustrated)	30
Winter, (Illustrated)	31
Brothers as Builders,	32
Two Vagrants,	33
When Winter Sets In,	34
Summer Days In Winter Time,	35
Not Done Ravin' Yet,	36-37
That Air New Womin,	38-39
Sharps and Flats,	40
That Fatal Day,	41
Evolution of a Name, (Illustrated)	42-43
One,	44-45
Song of a Storm,	46-47
To the Sunny South, (Illustrated)	48-49
Troubles the Year Around,	50-51
My Thanksgiving,	52
'Tis Christmas Just the Same,	53
The Blue-Jay and the Berry, (Illustrated)	54
Intemperance,	55
Here's to Chicago,	56
Ode to Autumn,	57
Salutes of Dawn,	58

BELLS. (Illustrated)	59 60 61
LIFE 'O JIM JONES,	62 63
LEAP YEAR VALENTINES,	64
A COLLOQUY,	65
A RINGER,	66
TWO DAYS,	67
THE STAR OF EMPIRE,	68
A MESSAGE OF HOPE,	69
LIFE'S HALF-WAY,	70 71
EAT 'EM AS YOU PICK 'EM, (Illustrated)	72
"BOY WANTED,"	73
THAT BABY BOY OF MINE,	74
PUBLISHED BY PEN,	75
A POINTER TO POETS,	76
THE CRIME OF SNOW BALLIN'. (Illustrated)	77 78 79
LOVELY MAY,	80
SPARE SPELLS,	81
OH VHERE ISH DOT PUP?	82
SONG OF THE INSTITUTE,	83
THE AUCTIONEER'S LAMENT. (Illustrated)	84 85 86 87
CALENDAR, 1898,	88
THE "OLD ORIENTAL,"	89
AN ECLIPSE ECLIPSED,	90
THEY SAW IT,	90
A SON OF THE SHADE,	91
A GUESS,	92 93
LINES TO A LEGAL LIGHT,	94
TWO CITIES,	95
EFFORT,	96
UNEARNED,	96
MEMORIES OF BOYHOOD,	97
ILLUSTRATION, (City of Lafayette)	98
LAFAYETTE,	99 100 101
ILLUSTRATION, (Home of my childhood)	100
TALE OF A BRASS KETTLE, (Illustrated)	102 3 4 5
TEN YEARS AGO,	106
IN MEMORIAM,	107
THE DYING TIME OF YEAR,	108 109

A SUMMONS,	110
DOWN THE VALLEY,	110
LINES TO HIS MEMORY, (Illustrated)	111
GONE WITH THE OLD YEAR,	112-113
IN HEAVEN ONE YEAR,	114
A SHINING MARK, (Illustrated)	115
CROWNED BY ANGEL HANDS,	116-117
ILLUSTRATION, (American Flag)	118
POEMS OF PATRIOTISM,	119
AN INQUIRY,	120
A "WAH" PROPHECY,	121
WEYLER WITH HER YET,	121
WILD NOTES OF WAR,	122
GOING,	123
APPROPRIATE EVERYWHERE, (Illustrated)	124
POSSIBILITIES,	124
TO HEROES OF THE SEA,	125
ODE TO CUBA'S FREEDOM, (Illustrated)	126-127
ILLUSTRATION, (The Bird of Freedom)	128
TO A BRIDE,	129
TEN LINES TO TEN YEARS, (Illustrated)	130
A MEMORY,	131
A BIRTHDAY WISH,	131
THREE MONTHS OF CHILDHOOD,	131
CLUBS,	132
TO A GRADUATING CLASS,	132
GO GATHER THE GEMS,	132
POETIC "FEET" DISPLACED,	133
A SEVERE STROKE,	133
SUSPICIOUS OF THE BRITISH,	133
DREAM OF THE TEACHER MAN,	134
WAYS OF THE WORLD,	134
THE WRITER AND THE FIGHTER,	135
REGULATED BY THE MOON,	135
EDITORS TAKE IT TOO,	135
TRIUMPH,	136
LIFE LINES,	136

Closing the sense within the measured time,
'Tis hard to fit the reason to the rhyme.
—*Dryden: Art of Poetry. II*

BUDS AND BLOSSOMS

No wreath of orange buds
  and blossoms fair
Adorns thy costume or
  entwines thy hair
To-day, as did a few
  brief years ago,
But in thy beaming smile
  love's radiant glow
Shines full as bright
  as when the bride
Pledged love for love
  whate'er betide;
And tho' some cares of life
  rest on thy brow,
Two buds of beauty
  and promise now
Unfold their blossoms
  'mid happy bowers,
To brighten and sweeten
  this home of ours.

SEVEN YEARS.

[December 27, 1894.]

How many years have passed away?
  How many seasons have come and gone?
How many returns of that bright day?
  How many cycles of time have flown?
    How many, dear one,
    How many have gone?

How many years since then have fled?
  How many days that make those years,
Of time gone by since we were wed,
  Have brought their joys, have brought their tears,
    Their cares and fears—
    How many years?

The mystic number seven surrounds
  My thoughts of time that's passed and gone,
And ties of home where love abounds
  Have grown in strength as years went on,
    And loved ones come
    To brighten home.

And many trials perchance we'll meet,
  Along the busy way of life,
But time's too short and life too sweet
  To count a care, permit a strife
    To enter life
    Of man and wife.

As we recount those passing years,
  That bring return of Christmas-tide,
Forget the cares, forget the tears,
  And number joys which were supplied
    Since man and bride
    Stood side by side.

A MOTHER'S LOVE.

From the distant home of the twinkling star,
From glittering realms where angels are,
From Pearly Gates where God's own stay,
An angel winged its peaceful way.

God sent the angel from Heaven above,
To find the fairest of His earthly love:
That angel came in lovely May
When skies were bright and world was gay.

During its mission 'mong earthly bowers
That angel entered a garden of flowers
Filled with the fragrance of blossoms fair,
And plucked the rarest and sweetest there.

As the angel from the garden passed
Its vision o'er a home was cast,
Where a babe's sweet smile and a mother's love
Were deemed as gems for Heaven above.

And the Angel gathered that Love serene,
The Flower it plucked, the Smile it had seen,
Caressed and cherished them all, and then
Spread its white wings for Heaven again.

As it arose to the Heavenly dome,
With fragrance and treasure of earthly home,
Of the Flower and Love and Smile it brought,
The Flower was fairest, the Angel thought.

But ere it reached that golden strand,
The Flower that had grown on earth so grand,
Had withered and fallen 'neath the Angel's feet,
And faded and gone was the Smile so sweet.

Vanished and lost were the Smile and Flower;
The Angel poised on Heaven's tower
With a Mother's Love, the theme and song
Of an angel host, of an angel throng.

The sweetest of earth or Heaven above
Is the precious theme of a Mother's Love;
It withereth not nor fadeth away
Like the smile of a child or flowers of May.

NOW.

Why brood and ponder
O'er things back yonder
Beneath the veil and misty cast
Of fallen tears
In by-gone years.
Along the trail of the dead past.
When "Now" doth need
Thy careful heed?

Why shouldst thou borrow
Aught from tomorrow?
Then break asunder that tearful tie
For sorrows fled
And hopes long dead
And buried under the years gone by:
Cease thy repine
When "Now" is thine.

The hour to fret
Has not come yet.
And time that's fled knows thee no more;
The fancied path
The future hath
Should not be tread so long before;
Then make thy vow
With naught but "Now."

THE CHILD.

Sun is hot,
   Heat of day,
Little tot
   Hies away;
Tireless feet,
   Playful hands,
On the street,
   In the sands;
Watchful care
   Of parents foiled,
Tangled hair,
   Dresses soiled;
Pouting lips,
   Streaming eyes,
Mamma whips
   And baby cries.

Perfumes rise
   In garden plots,
Baby spies
   Forget-me-nots;
There it lingers
   'Mong the bowers,
Dainty fingers
   Feeding flowers
To the bees
   The garden near,
'Neath the trees,
   Devoid of fear;
The bees—the why's
   Of baby's weep,
The sobs and sighs,
   Then soothed to sleep.

Tresses flying
  In the breeze.
Then espying
  Yonder trees.
Baby wanders
  To the woods.
Where it ponders
  Nature's moods;
Myriad throats
  In summer ringing.
The music notes
  From wildwood springing.
Glad and sweet
  The song-birds singing.
Joy complete
  To childhood bringing.

Leaves a-mingling
  With the snow.
Fingers tingling.
  Cold winds blow;
Dreamy nights.
  Days of noise.
Wild delights.
  Christmas toys;
Wintry days.
  Cosy nooks.
In-door plays
  And picture books;
Ever humming.
  Parlors ring
Till the coming
  Of the spring.

In realms above
   The angel smiles,
With radiant love,
   That love the child's:
The household bud,
   The blooming flower,
The sweet and good
   Of every hour:
The innocence,
   The hope, the smile,
The recompense
   Of care and trial:
The earthly gem,
   The joy of home,
The diadem,
   And Heaven's own.

THE SHIP OF LIFE.

Serene and calm in the harbor of youth
A Ship of Life at anchor lay.
Freighting its hold with knowledge and truth.
Gathering the ballast for a stormy way.

And on that Ship in the harbor calm
Two happy mariners were you and me.
As from its decks we looked beyond
And visions beheld but a stirless sea.

No cloud obscured the vaulted blue
As that good Ship turned out to sea.
That Ship so strong, and brave and true.
And all on board was joy and glee.

Our pilot guided that Ship away
With snow-white sail and stately mast.
And rocks and reefs that hidden lay
Were left in trackless paths of its past.

For many days this Ship of Life,
With prow turned toward a distant strand,
Sailed on in peace; nor angry strife
Disturbed the calm of a voyage grand.

But the captain saw a cloud arise
On the horizon of the blue,
And o'er the sea and o'er the skies
A fierce storm spread and mad winds blew.

Then angry waves did wildly play,
Our Ship was swept and swayed and tossed--
Its snowy sails were torn away,
And some of its stately masts were lost.

But a pilot true and captain brave,
And an ever faithful, valiant crew
Battled the adverse wind and wave,
And guided that Ship the tempest through.

   * * * * *

The Ship that sailed life's ocean wide,
And braved the fury of the blast,
Drifting with Eternity's gentle tide,
Has entered the Harbor of Peace at last.

FORGETFULNESS OF FATE.

When life unfolds like bloom of flowers,
And happiness doth crown his hours,
And rapturous scenes around him lie,
Man feels he was not born to die.

When brighter hopes with each day dawn
And new ambitions lead him on,
When fortune's star is shining high,
Man feels he was not born to die.

When man enjoys the zenith of his power,
He knoweth least the frailties of the hour,
And in his vain, exalted pride
Forgets that all before him died.

KEEP THE MAIN-TRAVELED ROAD.

How many there be who have drifted and swayed
From beaten paths, when they should have stayed.
In the traveled road with their burdensome load!
How many have wandered and lost their way
When lured to the wilds and led astray
'Mong dangers so rife on the road of life.
And out of the paths by their fathers trod
Have lost their hope and lost their God!

Turn not, O traveler, to paths that are new
And fraught with tangles awaiting you;
Turn not to the by-way, but keep on the high-way,
Let the main-traveled road e'er be your guide,
For near the path on either side,
Are countless cares and innumerable snares;
Shun them, O traveler, those thorns and the strife
That lurk in the shadows by the road of life.

While you're sustaining life's care-crowned load
Your safety lies in the main-traveled road;
While on life's rambles keep out of the brambles.
Turn not to the left nor turn to the right,
But press straight on with manhood might
'Long the highway grand that leads to the land
Where all is a gleam of childhood fair—
No poisonous shades nor wildwood there!

THE SUN-FLOWER.

OF stalwart strength
    And gallant length,
    And like a tree,
    It rises high—
    The great Sun-flower
    Whose blossoms tower
    Toward the sky—
The flower of flowers for me.

    While morning sun
    'Neath horizon
    Its light doth hide,
    This golden flower
    Turns its fair face
    With comely grace
    And waits the hour
To meet and greet its guide.

And as the brilliant orb of day,
That lights the world and all its way,
Pursues its path across the sky,
This stately flower that rises high
Above the sphere of other flowers,
(And like a dial to note the hours)
Unmindful of the blazing light
Nor dazed by splendor of the sight,
Careens its bloom with gentle grace
And views the sun fair in the face.

What other flower from morn till night
Endures the power of sun so bright,
And when the day comes to its close,
And all the world seeks sweet repose,
With stalwart form stands firm and true
To gather the drops of falling dew,
Or freshen its leaves in gentle rain
To greet the sun at morn again?
No flower of valley or mountain side
Is like the one the sun doth guide.

A THANKSGIVING PLEA FOR THE POOR.

The rich man may revel in a mansion grand,
And proffer the poor no helping hand,
But an unseen One will watch his way
And charge his account for Judgment Day;
But he who seeks to aid the poor,
To add a mite to their scanty store,
To answer the calls where poverty pleads,
Will receive reward for golden deeds.

Full many a hovel its own tale tells,
Where destitution and sadness dwells,
With the biting blasts of winter near
And the only warmth a scalding tear
That flows from a mother's saddened eyes
As she prays to Him beyond the skies
To help the dear ones left to her care,
And lighten her load of dark despair.

If you have aught for yourself, and more,
Go search the city from door to door
Till you find a home of the worthy poor
Where thoughts of kindness will long endure;
Let charity's strength be brought to bear
To break the pinions of poverty there,
And you'll be blessed in God's own way
For the good deeds done Thanksgiving Day.

LIFE'S SEASONS.

"Thou Art the Play-time for the World."

SPRING.

Bright morn of life, O Spring, with skies so fair,
The childhood of the year, exempt from care;
Replete with joy and happiness, O Spring,
Endeared art thou for pleasures that you bring.

Thy early songs of birds and hum of bees,
Thy flowers of field or plain and budding trees,
Combine their loveliness with hope and cheer
To make thee, Spring, the youth-time of the year.

Thy joys are bountiful indeed, and free,
Thou art the play-time for the world, and me.
Thy tears that flow are few, and they but seem
To fall to freshen flower or quicken stream.

SUMMER.

Successor thou of bright and vernal May,
The high and heated plane of life's mid-way,
Where all the wars of man are fiercely fought,
And all his victories are dearly bought.

Oh, season thou of toil-time and its strife,
Thy days are struggles 'mid the storms of life,
When man among a myriad of fears
Looks back upon his happy spring-time years;

And then in wonderment the future scans
For recompense of toil, reward of plans;
And brightening hopes at times flash thro' his tears
To paint a beauty scene on Autumn's years.

"*Oh, Season Thou of Toil-time.*"

"Thou Season that to Man Reward doth bring."

AUTUMN.

Oh, golden harvest time that lies between
The sultry storms of life and wintry scene;
The time when tinted foliage of trees
Is drifting down and onward with the breeze.

And if 'tis asked the fate of sons of men,
And what shall be the harvest gathered then;
"For some the weeds of woe, and blight and care
Is all the fruitage that is garnered there."

Thou season that to man reward doth bring
For thoughts and deeds in Summer and in Spring;
A golden time for all supplies to reap—
To watch and wait for that Eternal Sleep.

WINTER.

Oh Wintry time! thy frosts have killed the flowers;
The birds have flown from thee to sunny bowers.
Thy biting blast, and bleak and freezing breath
Hath come at last, and unto all is death.

That sparkling stream of life in childhood's days,
Congealed and silent now—its winding ways
Are drifted deep, and desolation rife
Hath spread o'er all, to mark the end of life.

The battles fought have made man brave for thee,
Oh, death! his spirit vision strong, to see
Beyond the beating, blinding storms you bring,
And view the splendor of Eternal Spring.

"The Birds have Flown from Thee."

BROTHERS AS BUILDERS.

If I should tell a brother to build,
    How and when and where, 'twould be,
Not as most of the world is willed,
    A temple on land or a ship on sea.

It would not be to build in massive piles,
    That tower toward the azure arch of sky,
With length and width a measure of miles,
    With steeple and dome full mountain high;

Nor with stately columns and marbled halls
    Lined with silver or adorned with gold,
Or beauteous frescoes to deck its walls,
    Like some rich palace of the kings of old;

But build ye brothers, as brothers should build
    A vast store-house of brotherly love,
And see that the same is abundantly filled
    From its uttermost depths to the skies above.

TWO VAGRANTS.

The Spendthrift flung his dollars far and wide.
The Miser clung to his, gold was his guide:
The Spendthrift at the end of life had naught.
The Miser but the gold that greed had bought.

And both were much despised by all good men:
        The Spendthrift pondered
          O'er fortune squandered
And sadly sighed to live life o'er again:
        The Miser lingered
        His cash and lingered
A while at Heaven's gate, then in despair
        He turned aside.
         (Admission denied)
For wealth could not gain him an entrance there.

No thought they'd given to life's most solemn side:
One lived in greed for gain—in want he died.
All disinherited by death at last—
And therefore both as vagrants should be classed.

WHEN WINTER SETS IN.

Some one'll be fooled 'long 'bout spring
When winter sets in, they will, by jing!
Needn't be expectin' this kind o' weather
To jes' linger 'long and hold out f'rever.

When winter sets in now purty soon,
And hazy lookin' rings wrap 'round the moon,
You can jes' look out, there'll be fallin' weather
One o' these days, 'taint far off ne'ther.

When winter sets in and winds begin to blow,
When it gets stingin' cold and you're shovelin' snow,
You'll wish you was down on the S'wanee river,
There or thereabouts, to stay f'rever.

When you see people goin' 'long the street
Shiverin' like a leaf and stampin' their feet,
And the north wind howls all the night through,
Whistlin' in the window half way into you

When winter sets in 'long 'bout spring,
And blizzards strike every livin' thing,
You'll wish somethin' else 'sides winter'd set in,
You'll wish nice days would come 'round ag'in.

SUMMER DAYS IN WINTER TIME.

When such warm days as some of these
   But afterglow of other season's time
Come saunterin' 'long with balmy breeze,
   A flirtin' like with winter time,
An' claimin' kin to fall an' spring
   An' changin' all of winter's ways,
It puzzles one to tell such things
   From bland-like, meek-eyed summer days.

This wearin' tints of Autumn's hours
   Instead of winter's robe of snow,
These out of season April showers—
   Why does the weather keep actin' so?
The storm king soon will come perhap
   All angered at this summer maid
A-lingerin' round on winter's lap,
   An' she'll be sorry that she stayed.

NOT DONE RAVIN' YET.

Dunraven came across the sea;
  He came, we guess,
After the cup which you and me
  As countrymen possess.

He brought with him an English yacht,
  An English tender,
And all the English fads he brought,
  To race Defender.

Those two fleet boats sailed out to sea
  For fifteen miles or more;
Valkyrie lost two out of three
  Uncorked his vials and swore

Dunraven did; his boat was beat
  Both out and back.
Defender's pace was most too fleet
  For British tack.

With frenzy wild, despair and wrath
   And froth and foam
Were scattered 'long the watery path
   He traveled home.

And now old "Dan" in wild commotion
   Still keeps his ravin' up.
While on this side of the old ocean,
   We simply keep that cup.

We fear not war nor battle's horde,
   Compared with he
When will that Englishman oh Lord!
   Done ravin' be?

Send word to that old English fop
   Whose talk has been so rough,
To just "haul in" his sails and stop
   His boat's not swift enough.

THAT AIR NEW WOMIN.

Oh, lands a-bloomin'! an sakes er-live!
How that air New Womin ever'll contrive
To take the place o' her ole man
An' reckon, an' figger, an' plot, an' plan
The way o' life all clean, plum through
Is more'n any wife I know kin do!

That air New Womin! oh, fiddlesticks!
Ye can't learn old dogs many new tricks!
I never 'low'd 'twas born in them
To be changin' jobs with thare ole men,
Fer wimin's place is 'long with man
Jist helpin' like, not leadin' the van.

I'm in habit o' speakin' out plain an' bold,
When a-talkin' to others o' the new an' old;
I'd let men manage the ships on the seas
An' fight men's battles 'bout as they please;
An' let 'em be 'tendin' to climbin' o' trees,
An' wimin the mendin' an' the quiltin' bees.

Some things thar be that 'peer mighty strange,
Seems goin' purty fur to make sich a change;
I've heerd it preached an' saw it writ with pen,
An' listened to 'em tell 'bout bein' born ag'in;
Wonder 'f that's the way one's got to pursue
When they git to be a real womin new?

The ole man an' me's been travelin' together
Not worryin' much 'bout wind or weather,
But jist sort a-keepin' in the main-traveled road,
Each helpin' to bear the other'n's load,
An' now we're comin' close down by the shore,
An' one of us two must soon go before.

We haven't time now fer things new-fangled,
Fer the lines of life might git all tangled,
If the drivin' was done by some new womin,
An' we'd miss the road that's buddin' an' bloomin'
With sweet smellin' flowers on most every hand,
An' leadin' straight on to Parydize land.

We've plodded 'long life's journey nigh through,
An' done the best we knowed how to do;
I want to be new when death calls me,
An' the only new womin that I keer to be
Is an angel womin, an' one o' that band
In world's a-comin' at God's right hand.

SHARPS AND FLATS.

'Gene Field wrote 'em, that's what he did
He didn't sign his name but he couldn't keep it hid
When he wrote of pollyticks or some "land-slide,"
An' told of the tricks that pollytishuns tried.

The only time 'Gene ever got badly mixed
With his "Sharps an' Flats," an' 'tween an' betwixt
The two couldn't tell just where he was at,
Was when he mistook a "Sharp" for a "Flat."

A fellow like 'Gene needn't sign any name
To tell who he is or build up his fame,
All of his readers throughout the broad land
Could tell when they saw his masterly hand.

I used to think that this 'Gene Field,
With the ready wit his mind could yield,
Should call 'em all "Sharps," an' let "Flats" be
For some other fellows not as sharp as he.

THAT FATAL DAY.

There's just one day in all the year
  When riches dare not show their head,
When naught but poverties appear,
  When all the men of wealth are dead,
    And all their cash's concealed away,
    The first of May.

That day, the one of all the year
  Of which assessors most inquire,
All men of riches do most fear,
  And some, perhaps, are wont to hire
    The same the year before 'twas said:
    "Not worth a red."

However strange that it may seem
  All men get poor the first of May;
At other times their riches teem
  And wealth flows free each other day
    But on that one brief day of spring
    They do not own a thing.

EVOLUTION OF A NAME.

When life began—an infant then
    And fads had not enthralled her-
She was a laughing little gem
    And MAGGIE'S what they called her.

When infant days had passed away,
    This little one to girlhood grew,
And 'long about her tenth birthday
    Just simple "MAG" was all she knew.

The spring-time of her life had come
    And she had known no troubles yet,
Except her name and thoughts of some
    Who called her MARG for MARGARET.

Another lapse of years I think
    Passed by—this maid had reached sixteen—
Her name likewise stretched out a link
    And took the form of MAGDALENE.

Sixteen—sweet time—right age you know
    And in this world of fads and fears
Quite old as girls e'er wish to grow—
    Therefore with caution count those years.

As time wears on what she calls life
    Becomes routine, each day the same,
And burdensome, 'less mid the strife
    There's evolution in her name.

This girl is now a graduate
    With great, wide sleeves and smile so sweet—
Upon her name doth hang her fate—
    She changes it to MARGUERITE.

And for a while the social whirl
    Employs this dear one gay and tall—
An ever blooming summer girl,
    With MARGUERITA for her call.

If she, perchance, some day should wed,
    Or cast a vote, or ride a bike,
With bloomers, she'd get it in her head
    To call it RITA, or the like.

And 'mong the droves of this girl's kind
    If you should ever meet a
"Coming Woman," perhaps you'll find
    Her name transformed to GRITA.

ONE.

One little one!
  That figure next to naught.
  What wonders hath it wrought!
What triumphs won!

Just one! of little things.
  And yet, indeed, how great
  The consequence   the caste of fate
That often clings

Around a single one
  In contests rife
  When races 'long the road of life
Are run, and won!

One little word set free
  Unbound the shackles of the slaves.
  One shot opened a thousand graves
The cost of victory.

One proudly chanted chorus:
  "My Country 'tis of Thee.
  Sweet Land of Liberty"
One flag waving o'er us.

One star it guided them
   By the twinkling light it gave
   To One who came the world to save—
The Star of Bethlehem.

And oh! one doom!
   That once for all awaits
   The shrouded mystery of fates!
One death! one tomb!

One life! one love
   To lead us on
   To one Eternity beyond
One Heaven above.

One life is done -
   We pass the portal
   Of realms immortal
And there abide with One.

SONG OF A STORM.

The sun had gone behind the hills.
A dusky twilight veiled the world.
It held the key to portals of the night
And bade the day depart.
I stood in wonderment and awe
Of nature's changeful scenes:
Above horizon 'rose a dismal pall.
At intervals a glimmering sheen
Of lightning sent its darting rays
Along the shapeless banks of blackness
And foretold the coming of a storm.
The air was solemn, sad and still.
And no sound broke the darkened calm
Save the cricket's chirp or locust's lonely song.
Or hurrying tread of feet
All homeward bound.

Then thunder's distant roar was heard.
And lightnings fiercer gleamed
And sent their vivid darts across the sky.
And nearer drew the storm;
Its breath fanned the forest and the field
And swept the grasses of the plain.
And to the city's inmost gates it came
And whirled among the streets and spires.

Then sudden broke the flood,
And torrents as they fell
Brought fright and fear to all:
And fierce winds blew and bent the boughs
Of sturdy oaks and elms
Until they kissed the earth,
Or bathed their verdure grand
In raging rivulets that ran.

The fierce blasts hurried on
And soon had passed:
The stately branches of the trees
That swayed, and sighed and sung
The harsh notes of the raging storm,
Had reared to lofty heights again:
The creatures of life who fled
From perils of the scene
To sheltered homes, came forth again
To view the lightning's glare that fainter grew,
And hear the distant knell—
Receding echoes of the storm's farewell;
And the moon threw its silvery tints upon
The curtain folds of darkness that had drawn,
And the sentinel stars of heaven shone
And sang their purest, sweetest song.

TO THE SUNNY SOUTH.

From out the bleak and frozen North—
Land of snow and wind, and storm and sleet,
Where all the wrath of elements meet,
Robbing the earth of its warmth and heat—
    We're flying forth,

Enroute to sunny, southern lands,
Where perfumed petals of blooming flowers
Ope wide their beauty 'mid sylvan bowers,
To lighten the hearts, to brighten the hours,
    Of happy bands.

Unlock your icy grasp, O frigid North!
Release your victims from snow-clad clime,
And bid them speed on swiftly flying time
From lands of prose to lands of rhyme
    To the Sunny South.

THE SUNNY SOUTH.

TROUBLES THE YEAR AROUND.

The coal man now is striving hard,
   His patrons one and all to please;
He sends around his little card
   Just after ev'ry little freeze.

His cards and coal are not the worst;
   They fill the bins and rob no till;
But every month the very first
   He sends around "a little bill."

As soon as winter thaws away,
   The ice man hauls his wagon forth,
And long before the first of May
   Is peddling extract of the north.

And while the ice man travels on
   The man of milk thinks it quite nice
To come along when he is gone
   And place some milk upon that ice.

You talk of men of ice and coal,
   The milk-man overshadows all,
The year around, exacts his toll
   Through winter, summer, spring and fall.

When winter comes and we've passed by
  The scorching summer's heated spell,
There is no longer need to try
  To cool the milk down in the well.

Think not when winter nears this man
  Of cows and cans and pumps and pails,
That aught outwits his mental plans
  That his invention ever fails.

With old Jack Frost he makes a deal
  To keep the cream that sticks to can
Sell only that which won't congeal
  The pure sky blue! oh heartless man!

The milk-man's days are not in vain:
  He's not in business for his health,
For he has water on the brain
  His route by water leads to wealth.

And sometimes there is something wrong
  Supposed of him; but hush! don't tell
He makes those strings a trifle long
  That hang those cans down in the well.

MY THANKSGIVING.

Thanksgiving day arrived again this year,
With joys of summer past and winter near;
The freezing winds had brought a message from the north,
The driven snows had come and covered all the earth;
I thought of days gone by and what they'd brought to me
As I had drifted out on life's uncertain sea;
But how to pass that day of thanks, and joy and glee,
And make it one of pleasure is what most puzzled me.
My thoughts turned to my home deserted, desolate,
The morrow seemed all crowned with darkest kind of fate
As I wandered lone and dreary along the street that night,
Keenly, sadly, feeling the sorrow of my plight,
And wishing for the presence of loved ones far away,
For cheering words of wife and the prattle and the play
Of those who brighten home with childhood's loving mien
In vain I tried to shorten the miles that intervene.
And through that sleepless night I struggled on
And plead release from such conditions till the dawn.
That marked the first approach of coming morn,
Brought new conclusions and thoughts new-born,
As bright as the day that with them came along,
As happy as the birds of spring-time song;
I thought of my old home, its joys and tears,
Of a good old mother and her burden of years.
And the hours were few that I had to wait
For a train that crossed to another state,
There my Thanksgiving this year was passed;
'Twas a joyous day, and its memories last;
The scenes of boyhood were revived and reviewed,
And the old-time paths retraced and pursued.
And this is the way I baffled the fate
Which shadowed the eve of Thanksgiving date.
When sad and lonely and loved ones are gone,
Just pass your Thanksgiving with mother at home.

'TIS CHRISTMAS JUST THE SAME.

The weather may be rough
An' the roads in very tough
Kind o' shape when Christmas gets around.
An' things not all a-movin'
In ways that you're approvin'
An' your lower lip a hangin' lower down
Than it ever hung before,
An' business mebbe poor,
Just because the people couldn't come to town;
But no one ain't to blame,
'Tis Christmas just the same.

If the creek's a playin' pranks,
Overflowin' uv its banks
On account o' rain a drippin' from the skies,
An' your corn's dirt cheap
An' you just hev to keep
Holdin' on a waitin' fer the price fer to rise
Tho' no market fer yer stuff
There's water quite enough
Without sheddin' more from a pair o' sad eyes;
There's no one much to blame,
'Tis Christmas just the same.

Then don't be a worryin'
As the time goes hurryin'
On, an' Christmas comes reg'lar once a year.
You'll live much longer
Grow better an' stronger
An' see more Christmases in your career
If you don't complain
Keep mud off the brain
An' your soul an' eyes keep bright and clear;
It don't matter much how Christmas came,
'Tis joyous Christmas just the same.

THE BLUE-JAY AND THE BERRY.

There was a jay-bird a pesky, squawky thing,
That sat on a bough in early spring
Watching the bloom in the berry patch
Impatient and eager a berry to snatch,

And on the morning of each new day
Would come the return of this blue-jay,
To perch on a tree near the garden gate,
To look and linger, to squawk and wait.

The housewife his habits quite well knew,
And rather suspicious of his presence grew;
She tried to rout him from the place
By planting a scare-crow with frightful face.

This jay-bird left that night in anxious mood,
Flew from the place where the scare-crow stood,
But before the berry to crimson grew,
That jay came back, and now the day through,

As if no fear he ever knew
Since he was hatched a bird of blue,
Sits on the arm of that scare-crow
Anxiously watching the berry grow.

INTEMPERANCE.

The greatest curse that lives today,
For ages past has held its sway,
And reigned as a despot with iron hand
In ev'ry clime and ev'ry land.
It enters circles fair and bright,
To sow a care, to spread a blight,
And seeking there to rule the hour
With its beguiling, conq'ring power.
It crowns the festal board with mirth;
Purports to be of dazzling worth;
Imbues each one who lingers there
With degradation and despair.
Its victim does not think so then
But tips his glass and drinks again.
When life's advanced he comes to grief,
But past all time to gain relief.

HERE'S TO CHICAGO.

Traverse the land from Tom Reed's state
　　To California's San Diego;
Coast all the shores from Behring's strait
　　To land-locked harbor of Pago-Pago,
Or travel a life-time at rapid gait,
　　You'll find no city like Chi-kay-go.

There is no place where councilmen are nested
　　Securely here below,
So steeped in sin, so fraud-infested,
　　No matter where you go;
And should Christ come, as Stead suggested,
　　He'd surely find it so.

ODE TO AUTUMN.

As the departing summer's glory fades
And frosts rest on the withering blades.
And much of the year is beyond recall.
There's a lesson of life in the leaves that fall.
In the changing scenes that meet the eye.
In the foliage hues and tints of the sky.
In the shaded lane or tree-lined street.
In the manner of all we see and meet.

Summer has gone with its joys untold
And its living green's transformed to gold.
What power so mystic, so wondrous strange
Has wrought such beauty amid this change
That pen of poet nor hand of art
Can ne'er portray the beauteous part.
Nor paint a scene to nature true
With the forest tinted a golden hue!

The autumn days that now are come
A melancholy time by some.
All sad and drear are said to be.
And oft they seem that way to me:
Their changing moods sometimes appear
The saddest of the passing year.
Yet idolized is autumn's day
That turns the green to gold and gray.

SALUTES OF DAWN.

I 'rose one morning at the break of dawn,
   Unlike I'd ever done for long before,
Because I always sleep till night's 'way gone
   And saw the streaks of day a-shooting o'er
The world, and lighting up the Eastern sky,
   And chasing back the sent'nels of the night,
Like sentinels are often made to fly
   When cov'ring some retreating army's flight.

And then a cloud I saw, a-hanging 'round
   And hov'ring close upon the horizon,
Not differing much in shape and looks from ground,
   Nor from the darkness that was hurrying on:
'Twas there to fortify the camp of night
   It seemed, tho' only for a brief, short spell,
Just long enough perhaps to set things right
   Give night a little time to say farewell.

Effulgent rays break o'er the waking world;
   For me it is a grand inspiring sight
To see those clouds of darkness backward hurled,
   And smiles of morn displace the dreams of night.
Oh grand the golden scenes of sunset sky,
   But more adored by me are those at dawn
When night, awakening, hastens its good-by,
   Amid salutes and echoes of the morn.

BELLS.

The bells! sweet bells that chime
At happy Christmas time!
That ring on every side
At joyous Easter-tide.

The poet tells
Of ringing bells,
Of funeral knells;
Of ancient chime,
Attuned to time
Of measured rhyme.

The bell! the bell!
High sounding bell
Whose echoes swell!
Oh bells so gladly ringing!
And bells! bells! bells!
Those mournful bells!
Those funeral knells!
Oh bells so sadly swinging!

The falcon's bell heralds its flight
And curfews tell of passing night:
And midnight's chime afar and near
Doth mark the time of passing year:
And "passing-bells" rang out of old
To sound sad knells—of death they told.

Bells! bells! bells! bells!
The bells! the bells!
Of all the bells
Which history tells,
There's one that rang at Liberty's birth,
And monarchs reeled
When its echoes pealed!
And dooms were sealed!
Most priceless bell of all the earth!

The bells! the bells!
Those jingling bells
Whose story tells
Of whitened fields on every side—
Of wintry climes,
Of Christmas chimes
And happy times,
As o'er the snow we gaily glide.

There is one bell
In annals of ages
Of which we sing,
Which poets tell
On history's pages,
That did not ring—
A curfew bell in Cromwell's time,
Suspended high in an ancient tower,
Each day wont to toll the curfew chime
And oft to note the end, the fatal hour
When life should take its final leave.
Within dark prison walls there lived that day
One o'erwhelmed by death's dark token,
And Cromwell's coming far away
Was all too late—sad hearts were broken
At thoughts of curfew to ring that eve.

"Curfew must not ring to-night!"
Cried out a maiden bold and brave—
Heroine of that belfry's dizzy height
A fate to rescue, a life to save!
And heeding not what dangers bring,
Muffled that bell's loud-speaking tongue,
(Unknown to the deaf old sexton far below)
And in that hour of frightful peril clung
To that bell wildly swinging to and fro
Her lover lived, for curfew did not ring!

The bells! the bells!
The wedding bells!
Which ring the joy of man and bride.
The bells! the bells!
The bright blue-bells!
That fadeless flower, fair Scotland's pride

The school bell tolling,
The school boy calling,
From paths of play he is prone to trod,
And those church bells,
The deep-toned bells,
Calling the sinner to the house of God.

The bells! the bells!
Jingling,
Tinkling,
Merry bells!
Swinging,
Singing,
Ringing,
Song-like echoes of some glad story
From birth-time hours to days of glory

Those auction bells,
And bovine bells
In all their harshness clanging:
Those breakfast bells,
And dinner bells,
And bells in belfries hanging;
Yes, all the bells
Which history tells
And poets have been singing,
Bring out those bells,
A thousand bells,
And set them all to ringing!

LIFE O' JIM JONES.

Jim Jones lived jes' sawin' wood,
An' Jim wuz jolly an' got 'long good.
You never seed Jim loafin' er layin'
Roun' s'loons, an' fergittin the payin'
Uv his onnus duze, an' like I know sum
Allus a-waitin fer sumthin' to cum
His way eezy. Jim worked hard.
I've seed him in meny er yard
Long 'fore roosters crode fer day
Nee deep in wood an' sawin' away
Thet's how Jim lived, an' Jim lived good
An' got all he had jes' sawin' wood.

Jim jined the Woodmin an' gess 'twuz thar
He lurnd his sawin' I don't know whar
Er why, er when it could hev bin
Er how he happund to begin
Ef it wuzn't then, but anyhow
Jim got to sawin', and I jes 'low
It wuz a lucky thing fer Jim.
An' thar's lots more jes' like him
A-wandurn' through the world today
Orter be nishiated jes' the same way;
It shakes 'em up an' does 'em good
To git 'em a-started sawin' wood.

I've often thot a feller like Jim
Set a good patturn, an' follurn' him
In his ever-day work a-sawin wood
I'd do a lot of fellers a hepe o' good.
Let 'em rise airly like Jim ust to
An' work till noon an' afternoon too.
On till nite till the cows cum home.
An' the ole turky gobler seeeed to rome
An' went to roost on a high-up lim'
With the turky hen settin' side o' him.
Thayde live longer an' do more good
Ef thay dun like Jim an' jes' sawed wood.

Jim lived long an' grode old
A-tryin to do what duty told.
An' whenever his advice wuz sought
Jim allus sed jes' what he thot
To young er old, an' told 'em to be good
An' reckermendid sawin' wood.
Jim wuzn't rich, er prowd, but sumhow
A thousan' luv'd him an' think o' him now.
When Jim went totterin' down the years
To his finul end, a milyun tears
Wuz shed an' Jim gained that reward
Jes' sawin' wood, an' trustin' in the Lord.

LEAP YEAR VALENTINES.

Soon the postman's arms will be
 Filled with love's sweet minstrelsy
While each waiting maid will pine
 For her leap-year valentine.
    —Detroit Free Press.

A DAY OR TWO LATER.

And in some postman's arms, perhap,
 The following Sunday night,
Or on some postman's lap,
 With lamps not very bright
Full many an arm-full sweet
 Sub-missive there reclines,
Enveloped quite complete,
 That leap-year valentine.

A COLLOQUY.

SON—"Mother, pray tell who was the man
　　Who first ordained the worldly plan
　　　To subdivide the year,
　　　So me and all my chums
　　Just have to wait and watch and yawn
　　Till all those tiresome months that on
　　　The calendar appear
　　Are nearly gone
　　　Before our Christmas comes."

MOTHER—"My son," the mother said "'tis nature's plan
　　　Perhaps, ordained by God and not by man."

SON—"Could not the days and weeks that fly
　　Count all the time for you and I
　　　From year to year
　　Without twelve months to interfere?"

Within this mother's mind there lurked a mortal fear
That argument once begun would last beyond the year,
For boys are boys—all this she knew before
And therefore wisely thought it best to say no more.

A RINGER.

Ring out the old, ring in the new:
Ring out the false, ring in the true:
Ring out the dark, ring in the light:
Ring out the dull, ring in the bright:
Ring out the slush, ring in the snow:
Ring in the swift, ring out the slow:
Ring in the good, ring out the bad:
Ring in the joyful, ring out the sad:
Ring out the night, ring in the dawn:
And ring! and ring! ring on! ring on!
Yes ring! and ring! for mercy's sake!
How much ringing does it take?
I think you've rung enough this pop,
So please ring off! ring off! and stop!

TWO DAYS.

Yesterday   a lovely day it was.
Pleasant because
   The world so seems
When the sun shines down
On a fettered, frozen town,
Softening the snow
And starting the flow
   Of tiny streams.

Yesterday   a pretty thing
Harbinger of coming spring
   Signal of winter disappearing.
Brightening the face of those
Awakening from long repose,
Inviting to birds with songs benign,
A safe, unfailing and certain sign
   That spring again is nearing.

Today   companion true
   Of yesterday
   And yesternight:
Skies all blue
   And fair and bright
   The spring-time way.

THE STAR OF EMPIRE.

"Westward the Star
  Of Empire takes its way"
And in that West-land
  Its wonders will display:
There potent power
  Will hold a sway,
And every hour
  Of every day,
Star of Empire, ascending higher,
  Apace with bright
    Progression's stride
  The world will light
    And lead and guide.

A MESSAGE OF HOPE.

x

To — —

As prison gates swing'in for thee,
And there deprived of freedom of the free,
A prison life it falls thy lot to bear.
Thy countrymen bid thee not despair.

Though prison walls upon thee frown
And prison garb bedecks thy form,
Outside those walls worse men than thee
Have gone unpunished by powers that be.

Though anxious hours disturb thy rest,
No felon's heart beats in thy breast,
Nor scornful hate of powers that be
Can rob thy right to liberty.

Then bravely bear that false decree,
Those shackles soon will fall—and free
Thy salient powers of speech and pen
Will plead humanity's cause again.

LIFE'S HALF-WAY.

At thirty-five I calmly pause today,
To view the place of life they call "half-way,"
And cast a retrospect o'er by-gone years,
Triumphs recount perhaps recall the tears.

I view the long decline up which I've come
Its rugged steeps, its rocks, its crags, and some
Of the weird ways through which I passed with fears,
Wond'ring if time has numbered half my years.

Is this meridian of man and life?
Doth it divide the share of joy and strife
Apportioned to allotted years of men
Who live to ripened age three score and ten?

The past is memory 'tis known to me,
But what the future holds what is to be,
Lies wrapt secure in shadows dark and deep,
And until reached that secret time will keep.

Oh by-gone years! the covering of thy ways
Has been uprolled to music of thy days,
But future time, if full of shining glow
Unknown its curtain still is hanging low.

Nor can we tell if we have reached the place
Which measures half of life's uneven race;
This numbering of the years is all divine
Perhaps more steeps before there comes decline.

Perhaps a plain, a great, broad table land,
On which repose full many glories grand,
Awaits the actor in the play and plan
Of years allotted to the life of man.

And should our pause be on the slope,
Or at the summit of the mount of hope,
Where man must say adieu to scenes behind
Begins the downward course of all his kind.

The brilliant rays of life's ascending sun,
That shone for me unto that summit won,
As down the long descent of life we glide,
Will shine as brightly on the other side.

Then what to you or I if swift or slow
Is the descent of life to vales below,
If passing scenes sublime and peaceful be,
And bright the sinking sun at eve we see!

February 22, 1896.

EAT 'EM AS YOU PICK 'EM.

You may talk of luxuries, luscious and sweet,
Of the fruits and berries that all love to eat,
And many fancy ways of fixing them up
In pies and preserves, in dish or in cup,
But as nature supplies them, oh give them to me,
Fresh from the vine, or fresh from the tree.
What suits the birds is good enough for me,
The berry from the vine or the fruit from the tree
The work of no cook in the can on the shelf
Can compare with the way I "can" it myself.
I'd sooner any time to get out and go
Where the juicy grape is hanging below
The vine as nature designed it, ripe and sweet
Tempting for all to pluck and to eat,
Than to have access to the sugared things
And the fancy luxuries of queens and kings.
You may have all the sweets that rest on the shelf
If you'll just let me do my "canning" myself.
Of the apple, the plum, the cherry that's fine,
Or the grape and the berry fresh from the vine.
What suits the birds is good enough for me,
Fresh from the vine or fresh from the tree.

"BOY WANTED!"

[The disappointing advent of the third girl in the Presidential household July 7, 1895.]

A sign hung on the door at Buzzard's Bay,
   And a flag from those "Gables" was flung,
And these were the words it was made to say
   And this was the song that most had been sung:
      "Boy wanted!"

     Yes, the flags were flaunted
     And the "Gables" were haunted
     By the song he chanted:
       "Boy wanted!"

When that little tot came to Buzzard's Bay,
   Announcing itself as "coming to stay,"
To adorn and brighten those Gables Gray,
   That sign from the door was taken away:
      "Boy wanted!"

     And now he is taunted
     For the song he chanted
     With courage undaunted:
       "Boy wanted!"

THAT BABY BOY OF MINE.

I cast my books and manuscripts aside one day
To listen to a prattling tongue of childhood gay,
To watch a pair of flying feet that sped their way,
And busy hands that strew disorder in their play,
    While guided by no thought but childish joy.

I caught that lovely form and pressed it close to me;
"WHOSE DARLING ONE ARE YOU?" I asked him to repeat;
With accents full of childhood's ways, in childish glee
There came from lips all wreathed in smiles so sweet:
    "ISE MAMMA'S BABY, PAPA'S 'ITTLE BOY."

    *   *   *   *

    Of bright and happy kind
  With face so fair, and sparkling eye
A wealth of worlds would fail to buy,
    That baby boy of mine.

Published by Pen:

For many days my wife's been hintin' 'round
   About some rhymes I wrote in days gone by,
   And ever' now and then she keeps inquirin' why
They can't be printed in a book an' bound.

Sometimes I think I'd kind o' like to do
   So just for her — no editor wants to see
   His scribblin' put in print — an' specially, me,
An' have the public all a scannin' through.

I s'pose some think a fellow with a printin' shop,
   An' lots o' type an' presses of his own,
   Unless his patronage is awful overgrown,
Might finish such a job before he'd ever stop.

But like the shoemaker who has no shoes
   It seems the printer's case is near a parallel,
   An' mighty hard it be to find sufficient spell
To do outsiders' jobs an' print the news.

So I've been thinkin' when I got time again
   To write them rhymes all scattered 'round,
   That she's been wantin' printed an' bound,
I'd simply publish them with my pen;

For somehow the writin' of one's own hand
   A charm to what's written does seem to lend,
   Better'n any type ever stood on end,
Better'n any printin' ever done in the land.

A POINTER TO POETS.

Here in our town two Majors live,
   Of wealth in mind and purse,
And these two Majors often give
   Some thought to riming verse.

The one composed a poem fair,
   'Twas several stanzas long,
'Twas written with the greatest care,
   And read by mighty throng.

The editor who gave it space,
   In mem'ry of the author's good intents,
When his pay-day came on apace,
   Sent forth his check for "forty cents."

The other Major at another time,
   Regarding "brevity" as the "soul of wit,"
Condensed the language of his rime
   And that same editor published it.

The man who gave these poems space,
   Admired the short one, and in rewarding it
Favored its author with kinder grace,
   And sent $3.00 for his "remit."

The moral of this tale is plain
   You shouldn't be long in discerning it
When penning poems relieve the pain,
   By using "brevity" for your wit.

Who knows but what the man who paid
   For these two poems which he bought,
His recompense would greater made
   Had neither poet written ought.

THE CRIME OF SNOW BALLIN'.

Suggested by the expulsion of seven school boys charged with throwing snow balls.

Things am gittin' so these new fangled days
You can't hardly live 'less you mend your old ways.
We ust to never go to deestrick schools
'Less we snow-balled—now you break rules
Ef you do sich things ag'in the teacher's say,
An' git sent home—sent there to stay.

When us old boys went to
 school long ago,
Many years back in the days
 I ust to know,
The teacher'd often jine our
 snow ball throw,
An' that teacher's face we'd
 wash in the snow.
But he didn't turn us out for
 nuthin' like that
Ef we all studied good an'
 got our lessons pat.

Wonder what the Lord specks to do with the snow
Ef it aint made for boys to wad up an' throw.
We ust to all use it for sleighin' an' throwin',
Now the wind jes' hez it to use when a blowin':
It's that way now—the world an' its ways
Hev changed a mighty heap since our school days.

I can well remember when a
 whole pack
Of us school boys would all
 take a whack
At a feller passin'—the balls
 'u'd jes' fly,
An' a dozen mebbe hit him
 'fore he got by;
But we wusn't sent home for
 things like that
Ef we all studied good an' got
 our lessons pat.

We ust to build forts an' put armies in 'em
An' when the other boys would run up ag'in 'em.
We'd take some icy balls (of course jes' in fun)
An' pelt 'em hard an' fast till ev'ry feller'd run;
But if we studied good and got our lessons pat
They'd never spell a feller for things like that.

We'd make our bullets out o' real soft ice
(An' leave 'em out nights to freeze hard an' nice)
With hunks o' coal in 'em er some sich stuff
That'd sometimes hurt ef throw'd hard 'nuff;
But they never turned us out fer nuthin' like that
Ef we all studied good an' got our lessons pat.

Oh, what queer stages our larnin's passin' through,
An' what a purty fix we're gittin' into!
What in the world will the boys all do
Ef they can't play a bit—when they spell 'em ef they do?
It's that way now for the world an' its ways
Hev changed a mighty heap since our school days.

LOVELY MAY.

I met a friend as I walked the street,
  One dreary, dismal April day,
  Who longingly wished for Lovely May.
I said to that one I chanced to meet,
  To lighten his heart and brighten his way,
  "We're traveling on toward Lovely May."

What if the clouds are bleak and dark
  And chill the winds that blow today!
  We're hastening on toward Lovely May.
Tomorrow may hear the song of the lark,
  Or the note of the robin and the jay;
  We're hastening on toward Lovely May.

Then why regret these April showers
  Which overspread the skies today!
  We're hastening on toward Lovely May
Where song of birds and bloom of flowers
  Will make world bright and glad and gay;
  We're hastening on toward Lovely May.

SPARE SPELLS.

I've written rimes
At short, spare spells
I found in life as years went on;
Ah! no one tells
Just whence they came, just where they've gone—
Those idle spells,
Life's odd, spare times.

I've written lines
As Riley said in a sweet rime
His pen inscribed one day
"To lure the length'ning miles into
The pleasant Afterwhiles," and through,
To joy's confines
To after years where smiles greet time
And sorrows fade away.

Since I begun,
And time has onward passed,
Some I have penned
To foe and friend,
And some to loved ones in my home;
To them these rimes,
Of odd, spare times,
Are joyful chimes
And songs of pleasure as they come,
That still will sing
And chime and ring
When I am gone at last—
When life is done.

OH VHERE ISH DOT PUP?

✣

To commemorate the following advertisement: "Dog lost. A small *white* pup, with black ears, and some *white* on tail."

Oh vhere, oh vhere is mein vhite pup shmall,
   Vot I tried to vind him so hard und vail,
He vas all over vhite mit some leedle plack ears
   Und some more vhite on his leedle vhite tail.

Oh vhere, oh vhere is mein leedle vhite pup
   Vot did got lost und didn't back come,
He vas all over vhite from his het clean up,
   Mit some spot on his ears und tail vhite some.

Oh vhere, oh vhere do dot leedle pup sthay?
   Oh vhere dis world in has doggy all gone?
Dot leedle vhite pup vot has vandered avay,
   Und some more vhite mit his tail vas on.

Oh vhere, oh vhere is mein vhite dog lost,
   Vot in der paper I did atvhertise,
Und paid for some money und never run crost
   Mein leedle vhite doggy mit vhite in his eyes
Und lots more vhite on his tail for its size.

SONG OF THE INSTITUTE.

There is no state like Illinois,
There is no place like Iroquois:
Oh land of corn, and flowers and fruit!
Oh home of the farmers' institute!
I labor hard throughout the year,
And when I've plucked the golden ear,
I do my chores and then I scoot
Right into town to the institute.

CHORUS.

Oh let me live in Illinois!
Oh let me stay in Iroquois!
And 'tend the farmers' institute
The institute! tu-tute! tu-tute!

When frost is on the pumpkin and corn,
The farmer's out at early morn,
A-gath'ring in the golden fruit
That takes the prize at the institute.
It was not many years ago
When things moved 'long most awful slow,
But now they're going lick-et-y scoot
And the candidate's at the institute.

CHORUS.

I don't like none of your western galoots
In rattle-snake hats and leather suits
Or the city chaps a "shootin' the chutes"
I 'tend my farm and the institutes.
I don't like none of your whistles shrill,
Or toots that blow at the knittin' mill,
And none of those Watseka shoots
Who go to Crescent to get their toots.

CHORUS.

THE AUCTIONEER'S LAMENT.

My callin's been ailin' an' I'm chuck full o' fears
That this "cryin'" occupation will soon turn to tears.

THE AUCTIONEER'S LAMENT.

Sales hev bin few for sev'ral years,
You seldom ever hear the cry uv auctioneers;
My callin's bin ailin'-an' I'm chuck full uv fears
That this "cryin'" occupation will soon turn to tears.
    Yes, bizness hez been ailin'
      Since these hard times come on,
    An' my occupation's failin',
      It's goin'! goin'! gone!

The people don't 'peer stingy—but many aint ez free,
An' somehow hopes are dingy—there's no joy an' glee
Ez I look through my tears an' fancy I can see
Back not many years when 'twuz different fer me.
    It's no longer now smooth sailin'
      Since these hard times come on,
    An' my occupation's failin',
      It's goin'! goin'! gone!

I've often wondered, an' figured with a will
Ef some one blundered, an' managed fer to kill
The bizness tryin' to enlarge it, an' figured on until
I jes' conclude to charge it to the Dingley bill.
    Fer bizness hez bin ailin'
      Since these hard times come on,
    An' my occupation's failin',
      Goin'! goin'! gone!

A few years ago, ever' day most,
I us't be called to sell off a host
Uv furniture an' fixin's, an' wagons an' teams,
An' a thousan' things, but since then it seems
    My bizness hez bin ailin'
      Since these hard times come on,
    An' my occupation's failin',
      It's goin'! goin'! gone!

I us't to sell hogs, an' calves and cows,
The household dogs, an' the stirrin' plows,
An' all the traps known to human invention,
An' some other things "too num'r'us to mention."
    Since then bizness hez bin ailin',
      Fer these hard times come on.
    An' my occupation's failin'
      It's goin'! goin'! gone!

With sales gittin' few fer sev'ral years
An' nuthin' to do fer the auctioneers,
An' nuthin' to sell, none able to buy,
'Taint no use to yell, an' no use to "cry."
    Fer bizness hez bin ailin'
      Since these hard times come on,
    An' my occupation's failin',
      Goin'! goin'! gone!

    *   *   *   *   *

When Uncle Jim Parker moved into town
He quit cryin' sales an' settled down;
Fer many a year he hezn't bin heard,
Ez an auctioneer, to utter a word.
I wonder'f he on general suspicion
Expected the change in bizness condition?
Wonder'f he knew there'd be hard sailin'
Fer the auctioneers an' bizness be failin'
Ez soon as hard times got to comin' on,
An' the occupation'd be nigh most gone,
Then quit auctioneerin' a livin' to earn?
Great head uv hiz, to call sich a turn!

Ef times keep gettin' worse what'll we do
Fer a livelihood? Jes' "cry" says you?
If you ever listened to John Bailey's tone
A hull day through, er heard Harve Stone,
Er ever stood under the fiery yell
Of Dave McFadden er Robert Mell,
Er an auctioneer that's Dunn by name,
Er "Col." Sam Stone uv Danforth fame,
You'd lend an ear to my mournful tale
An' not appear to greet an' hail
The present year, with hard times on,
An' the auctioneer's best days all gone.

This is one uv our "way-off" years.
And toler'ble tough on the auctioneers,
An' rough on the chaps who print bills too,
But I guess, perhaps, we'll both pull through.

Ez the farmer to his farm is hangin' on
An' my occupation's goin'! goin'! gone!
Ez this is one uv our "way-off" years.
Let's auction off the auctioneers.

*   *   *   *   *

And while amazed at this suggestion bold,
The hammer fell   "Once! Twice! and Sold!"

CALENDAR, 1898.

	Sunday	Monday	Tuesday	Wednes.	Thursday	Friday	Saturday		Sunday	Monday	Tuesday	Wednes.	Thursday	Friday	Saturday
Jan...							1	July...						1	2
	2	3	4	5	6	7	8		3	4	5	6	7	8	9
	9	10	11	12	13	14	15		10	11	12	13	14	15	16
	16	17	18	19	20	21	22		17	18	19	20	21	22	23
	23	24	25	26	27	28	29		24	25	26	27	28	29	30
	30	31							31						
Feb...			1	2	3	4	5	Aug...		1	2	3	4	5	6
	6	7	8	9	10	11	12		7	8	9	10	11	12	13
	13	14	15	16	17	18	19		14	15	16	17	18	19	20
	20	21	22	23	24	25	26		21	22	23	24	25	26	27
	27	28							28	29	30	31			
Mar...			1	2	3	4	5	Sept...					1	2	3
	6	7	8	9	10	11	12		4	5	6	7	8	9	10
	13	14	15	16	17	18	19		11	12	13	14	15	16	17
	20	21	22	23	24	25	26		18	19	20	21	22	23	24
	27	28	29	30	31				25	26	27	28	29	30	
April...						1	2	Oct...							1
	3	4	5	6	7	8	9		2	3	4	5	6	7	8
	10	11	12	13	14	15	16		9	10	11	12	13	14	15
	17	18	19	20	21	22	23		16	17	18	19	20	21	22
	24	25	26	27	28	29	30		23	24	25	26	27	28	29
									30	31					
May..	1	2	3	4	5	6	7	Nov...			1	2	3	4	5
	8	9	10	11	12	13	14		6	7	8	9	10	11	12
	15	16	17	18	19	20	21		13	14	15	16	17	18	19
	22	23	24	25	26	27	28		20	21	22	23	24	25	26
	29	30	31						27	28	29	30			
June..				1	2	3	4	Dec...					1	2	3
	5	6	7	8	9	10	11		4	5	6	7	8	9	10
	12	13	14	15	16	17	18		11	12	13	14	15	16	17
	19	20	21	22	23	24	25		18	19	20	21	22	23	24
	26	27	28	29	30				25	26	27	28	29	30	31

FIGURES OF THE NEW YEAR.

The old, departing, unto new gives place,
And tho' no animation on the face
Of characters so silent and so dumb,
They tell the story of a year to come;
For all the types assembled in this plate,
Are sentinels of time, and hope, and fate.

THE "OLD ORIENTAL."

You may talk all you please
Of the Woodmen degrees,
Of the wood and its sawin',
And the buckin' and pawin'
Of the old stubborn goat,
And his buttin' by note;
Of his startin' and goin',
Of his stoppin' and throwin',
And tell of the fate
Of the poor candidate
In tones sentimental,
But the most detrimental,
Is the fun incidental
To the "Old Oriental."

AN ECLIPSE ECLIPSED.

There was an eclipse the other night
And thousands awaited with anxious delight
To see old Luna's face all hid from view
While passing earth's dark shadow through;

It was to be total a great, grand sight,
And many prepared to stay out all night;
But 'twixt cup and lip there are many slips
The storm cloud eclipsed that great eclipse.

THEY SAW IT.

"Where were you last evening dear?" her mother said.
"I looked in vain for you my dear before I went to bed
And thought to press a good-night kiss upon those ruby lips.
I quite forgot there was to be a moon's eclipse."

"Yes, mother dear, that same event escaped my mind
Till Charley came and asked were I inclined
To go with him to view the moon's, great, grand eclipse;
It was delightful mother I took along my lips."

A SON OF THE SHADE.

He lies in a hammock enjoying the breeze
With all the comfort and all the ease
Of a don't-care-for-nothing and go-as-you-please
Sort of a way   in the shade of the trees.
    Just seeing what he can see,
    Unmindful of hours that flee.

The birds are nesting in the trees.
He hears the hum of the busy bees.
And out in the garden, with rolled up sleeves
And hoe in hand, his dad he sees.
    His dad was born to work with a vim
    He'd sooner 'twas dad than him.

Things he likes most are shady trees,
And a hammock swinging in the breeze,
Lazily loafing there at ease
With nothing to do but do as you please.
    "No sun a shinin' hot and high
    On me," says he, "I'd sooner 'twas dad than I."

A GUESS.

MYSTERY OF THE CHICAGO RECORD'S PRIZE STORY.
"SONS AND FATHERS."

✱

> "As sometimes in a dead man's face,
> To those that watch it more and more,
> A likeness hardly seen before
> Comes out—to some one of his race."
> —*Tennyson's "In Memoriam."*

I pursued the story of "Sons and Fathers,"
   And on the "mystery" laid mighty stress,
But there's one little thing that bothers:
   "Only women and girls may guess."

'Tis a lesson of life, of hope, and love,
   Of envy and hate and cumbrous care,
But jewelled with light from the heavens above,
   And couched in language chaste and rare.

Out of the tangle of plot and plan
   Comes a solution I believe that wins
I figured it out as the story ran
   That Edward and Gerald are certainly twins.

There at the church as the storm beat wild,
   Where women sought shelter that terrible night,
One bearing a "coffin" 'tis said, for a child,
   And a great white bird there fluttered in fright.

Was a man we divine as Gaspard Levigne:
   And Marion's pale face in the lightning's glare:
And the "coffin" she carried but a violin:
   And Rita who rescued that creature so fair.

"Cambia," for beauty and talent in two worlds known,
   Who smothered her sorrow in the music of years,
Who searched long and vain for records flown,
   And honored a grave with flowers, and her tears.

Is happy again—her angel face once more
   Is shorn of sadness and a sweet-toned voice
Is singing the songs of the years of yore,
   And a son, and mother, and father rejoice.

For Edward and Mary the clouds have rolled by:
   His past is revealed and their visions behold
A future of promise—on the storm-rent sky
   Is a rainbow rich in the tints of gold.

There is one thread of this mystery tale
   That is hopelessly lost, and amid my despair
I guess that all guesses summarily fail
   To tell what become of sweet Kitty Blair.

Oh, should the readers of stories like this,
   With all its plot and plan and thought,
A million of miles the mystery miss,
   The world is better for the good it taught.

LINES TO A LEGAL LIGHT.

[On the occasion of the marriage of Mr. Frank L.
Hooper, September 29th, 1891.]

Your "case" is "one" it now appears,
Not by demand for excessive "fees,"
But by seven, long, consecutive years
Of ardent, strong, persuasive "pleas."

No "writ of replevin" was ever issued,
No "change of venue" ever taken
Faith in the "justice" of your "court"
Throughout the "suit" remained unshaken.

Let us "brief-ly" ask in an "abstract" way
That no "appeal" of the "case" be made;
Frank-ly submit (with modest Grace)
To the happy "verdict" so long delayed.

If in after years, in your home "pur-suits,"
Troubles and "trials" should ever arise,
Endeavor to "quash" all such disputes,
Or settle the same by "compromise."

That good wife of yours "seek to retain-'er"
As long as you "argue" with "legal" breath,
And bestow the love you bestowed to gain her;
Let the only "divorce" be the one by death.

TWO CITIES.

[Frankfort, Indiana, 1885.]

Today I rest on a shady slope,
Enjoying life and health and hope;
The trees are swaying to and fro,
The grass and flowers are bending low;
Visitors enter with silent tread
To view this city of the dead.

Around this sacred spot enclosed
Another city lies, and much disposed
To wealth, activity and life,
Engaged in busy, worldly strife,
Filled with toil and noise and din,
Contrasting widely from this I am in.

Many a one from a pleasant home
Views that city's stately dome,
And many attentive listening ears
Will hear the sound, in future years,
Of its huge clock, like a deep-toned bell,
Bidding the hours and days farewell.

And many a tear which flows from thought
Of grief and sorrow there, is brought
From the living city year after year
To moisten the flowers that are planted here.
These cities are linked by time that's fled—
One for the living and one for the dead.

EFFORT.

If there looms up a task before you
 Like mountains high,
So tall it seems that it extends
 From earth to sky,
And you'd remove it, we implore you
 Not stand and sigh,
Nor wait until your worldly ends
 Have gone awry,
Then call for aid—all will ignore you
 And naught reply,
For much of life's success depends
 On how we try.

UNEARNED.

Some men who fish and catcheth naught,
Make much display of fish they've caught;
And all the honors some have got,
Are those they've stolen or they've bought.

Memories of Boyhood.

LAFAYETTE.

A proud city stands
   On the banks of a stream.
Whose waters and sands
   In the sunlight gleam,
And my memory fills
   With thoughts that are fair.
Of the homes on the hills
   And the highlands there.

O'er that broad stream
   Three structures span.
Where train and team
   And child and man.
In ceaseless throng,
   Pass early and late
With commerce strong
   For the "Star" of state.

To the northward lies
   A field of fame,
Where standards rise.
   Where a chieftain came
With a warrior band
   At night-time hour,
And avenging hand
   For vanishing power.

My thoughts are turning
   To by-gone times,
To a seat of learning—
   I hear its chimes
Just across that river
   Where nobly stands
That gift of a giver
   With generous plans.

The home of my childhood
  Lies just beyond
Where field and wildwood
  All blend in one;
Where sweet-scented blades
  Of meadows are found.
And the sylvan shades
  Of forests abound.

Far into the woods
  I was wont to roam
'Mong nature's moods,
  In nature's home.
And my soul oft stirred
  By the tinkling bells
Of the wandering herd
  Through vales and dells.

And the bird's sweet song
  At dawn of day.
As I passed along
  Some woodland way.
Where nature rejoices
  With heart light and free.
Would waken the voices
  Of nature in me.

As the sun sank low
  At the close of day,
'Mid the evening's glow
  I'd wend my way
Where no sound floats
  On the air above
Save the mournful notes
  Of a cooing dove,

Or the lonesome song
  Of the whip-poor-will
As it floats along
  The lowland and hill,
And the clock of the town
  From its massive tower
With deep-toned sound
  Would note the hour.

Oh city of fame,
  Thou art dear to me.
Revered thy name,
  And scenes environ thee.
Of field and grove
  And forest and plain.
And I long to rove
  Their paths again.

TALE OF A BRASS KETTLE.

O, while you're talkin' of boyhood ways,
    Of capers an' pranks of youth's delight.
An' tellin' your tales of long-ago days,
    When pants was short an' hair was white.

Just listen to me, it's a way-
    back date
Concernin' which I'm goin'
    to tell.
'Twas out'n White County in
    the Hoosier State
An' 'bout a brass kettle
    that sank in a well.

It must o' been back in the 60's somewhere
    When we lived far out on a prairie farm
With a hut for a home, and neighbors rare,
    An' the coyotes soundin' their wild alarm..

With a mighty slim start an' the country all new
    Many years yonder in days of yore.
Father an' mother had all they could do
    To keep the gaunt wolf away from the door.

'Twas on a warm day 'long late'n the spring.
    An' father was plowin' in the field alone.
Can't just remember the date o' the thing
    On account o' the years that's passed an' gone.

The day was bright an' the sun shone fair,
    And father was plowin' like "sixty-three."
An' mother'd gone an' left me to care
    For two little tots both younger'n me.

We played all 'round an old corn pen,
    On the shady side most, for the sun was hot,
An' under some rails that stood on end
    Down close by the old stable lot.

The day I remember and where we were at,
    We three—a baby sister an' brother, an' he
Not much older'n her, an' blind at that—
    They made just two—an' the other'n was me.

Poverty perched on the rails o'erhead.
    An' luxuries scarce 'round that old corn bin—
'Twas just take some water an' a crust o' bread
    An' then go to rompin' and playin' ag'in.

An' I done my best most all the while,
    Though the sun was hot and the shade was slack
'Round that corn pen an' that old rail pile,
    To keep 'em satisfied till mother got back.

Of the bread an' water that was our lot,
    Whichever they wanted I tried to get
Whether they needed it much or not,
    An' the little brass kettle is a memory yet.

I took that treasure of many a year,
  Of which my mother had often told,
An' hied away to a well that was near,
  With boyhood daring brave and bold.

I lifted the cover rude and
    plain
  That shut out the heat o' the
    sun's bright glow,
As I'd seen done, yes time and
    again,
  An' swung it down to the
    water below.

I pressed on the pole—a forked limb
  Which had been fixed in place of a string,
And the water rushed over its polished brim,
  Until it filled an' sank the thing.

But when I 'rose to lift my prize
  An' bear it upward with a forked limb,
Just then it was that a boy my size,
  Found that a kettle had deserted him.

Lost! sunk to rise no more! I reeled
  In fright, and uttered one loud yell
To break the news to father in the field!
  "The little! brass kettle!! is in the well!!!"

An' brother Reed an' sister "Lib"
  Who'd caught the anguish of my spell,
Sat down an' sobbed by the old corn crib;
  "'E 'ittle b'ass tittle, i' fell in 'e well!!"

THE RACE TO THE FIELD.

As if a life was hanging by a thread
    And final fate depended on my flight,
With whitened face and hatless head.
    I flew to the field with my all my might.

    Across the furrows with wild acclaim
        An' over the clods I stumbled and fell
    And from my lips in anguish came.
        "The little! brass kettle!! is in the well!!!"

Far into the field was heard my scream
    Inaudible, and yet my frightened spell
Borne on the breeze to parent ear did seem
    Like news of death! of drowning in a well!

With heart in mouth and apprehension dire,
    A race for life of one he loved began,
And o'er and through that field with soul afire
    At desperate speed to reach that well he ran.

There anxious eyes gazed down to waters calm—
    No circumstance of death to start sad tears—
But heart-sick from fatigue, and strength undone,
    That race brought him a frightful weight of years.

What fearful havoc oft is wrought by storm!
    What strength is lost by labor overdone!
What thoughtless acts in youth we all perform!
    What fateful steps before life's race is run!

TEN YEARS AGO.

[February 27, 1887.]

Dear Friend—oft-times I think of long ago:
(Time is eventful, and changes so)
Ten years backward shall memory turn
To glance o'er youth-time and efforts to learn
Some lesson at school! I was there, you know.
      Ten years ago.

The halcyon days of boyhood are past:
Let memory recall them, for while it doth last
'Twill ever recount them to sift some bright ember
From ashes of years I so fondly remember—
Memory tonight is whispering low,
      Ten years ago.

Why is it, dear one, I cannot refrain,
And why, furthermore, do you never complain
Of reading the products of my feeble pen
That tell of those years again and again?
And now is reviewing with rythmic glow,
      Ten years ago.

Ten years ago! why now it seems to me
That more than yesterday it cannot be,
When I with boyish mind and heart began
To involve myself in love's sweet plan,
And write those missives now cherished so,
      Ten years ago.

By affection's grasp in youthful days,
My heart was bound in loving ways:
And on my pen a great encumbrance laid;
Nor shall it rest until thou'rt paid—
Sweet debt of love, I first began to owe,
      Ten years ago.

In Memoriam.

"THE DYING TIME OF YEAR."

[To the Memory of Eugene Field.]

The days were bright and heavens clear,
But there was a sound in the forest near
Whose echo fell both sad and drear
    On the listening ear:
    'Twas the rustling leaves
    In the autumn breeze
    All nature sighing,
    Crying,
    "This is the dying
      Time of year."

A home was filled with loving light,
The lamp of life was burning bright,
No thought of the spirit taking flight
    From one so dear
    But hark! without
    All 'round about,
    The sad winds sighing,
    Crying,
    "This is the dying
      Time of year."

No thought of death's angel silently creeping
That night where our poet was calmly sleeping.
No sign nor omen of loved ones weeping.
    No thought of a tear
   To bring relief.
   To break the grief
   Of scenes of death so trying
   No sighing—
   Simply the dying
     Time of year.

Through ages progressive since worlds began.
No words more impressive were spoken by man.
Nor faithful allusion to nature's great plan.
    No thought more dear:
   The breezes passing.
   Each other caressing.
   And leaves down flying.
   Sighing.
   All tell of the dying
     Time of year.

A SUMMONS.

It was no crushing weight of years
  That summoned the soul of a noble wife,
But an unkind call of the Reaper Death
  Ere she had reached the noon of life.

DOWN THE VALLEY.

  Down death's dark valley,
  We're going "one by one;"
With faces all turned toward the setting sun,
A great human throng, since the world begun.

  Down, down that valley,
  Has glided "one by one."
That road will be traveled till the race is run,
And life's procession ends—The world is done

  When all down the valley
  Have passed "one by one."

LINES TO HIS MEMORY.

[William Wallace Gilbert, died April 15, 1897.]

His life to hope gave newer birth
  As bright as sunshine from the sky,
And no reminder of his worth
  Can song or elegy supply.

No ill to man e'er filled his heart
  Nor unjust deed e'er dimmed an eye,
But sorrow played a dismal part
  When God decreed this man should die.

The tender ones of childhood know,
  Adore and love his kindly ways,
And faltering forms of age bestow
  A fulsome gratitude and praise.

A hamlet mourns—and hundreds more
  Have shed a tear or breathed a sigh,
And 'mid this sadness all deplore
  That one so good and true must die.

The sorrowed homes of grief and tears,
  That now seem cheerless, drear and cold,
Will brighter be in coming years
  As his life story oft is told.

GONE WITH THE OLD YEAR.

[Miss Mary Wall, Burton, Indiana, died New Year's eve, 1885.]

Hark! the requiem of the dying year,
With mournful sound to many an ear,
Is borne aloft; its plaintive cries,
Appear ascending toward the skies,
Where dwells, whence comes this mystic power
That so surrounds and desolates the hour!

O, why should we in sadness bow today,
E'en though our hopes pass unfulfilled away,
And love is changed to hatred and to scorn,
Why not enlist to greet the New Year's morn
As a noble harbinger of joyful mien,
That fills each heart with boundless hopes serene?

Alas! the death knell of the parting year
May toll and toll again, time sheds no tear,
But when the door of death swings open wide
And bids a dear one through his portals glide,
'Tis sad to contemplate such scenes of grief
And vain to search for measures of relief.

Time in its flight speeds boldly on and on,
The glimmerings of the eastern horizon
Dispel the dismal darkness of the night,
Betokens the return of day aright;
But light or splendor scenes that there abound,
Cannot dispel the gloom that lurks around.

O bright New Year, why so unmindful thou,
Of woes that flood our minds and hearts just now?
Oh let your light so graciously given,
Transmit the smiles of merciful Heaven,
Tell us the one that we so sadly miss
Has reached another, better world than this.

Upon the morrow of that day so fair,
All cumbered with a load of deep despair,
And 'midst the unkind fall of chilly rain,
Moved forth the solemn, silent fun'ral train;
Yes, moved with mournful, melancholy tread,
And gently laid dear Mary 'mong the dead.

No more in life we'll greet her smiling face;
But time, while mem'ry dwells, cannot erase
Her noble qualities of heart away,
So strong the sorrowed impress of today.
O "Precious Faith" that guides her safely o'er,
Direct our barque to that celestial shore.

IN HEAVEN ONE YEAR.

One glance backward on memory's tide,
Tells us the day that Frankie died,
And speaks of his entering that Heavenly way,
One full, long year ago today.

Why view that day as one of sorrow and despair,
And why encumber life with loads of care,
Or cast one sigh or shed one tear,
When Frankie's been in Heaven a year?

Such things as days or years of earthly clime,
Are unnumbered and unknown to Heavenly time;
And pray what worth would be a day or year,
When time is unending and eternal there?

Upon his grave let blossoming flowers
Impart a sweet fragrance to lonely hours,
And while earthly years to you are given,
Just count them all as time for him in Heaven.

A SHINING MARK.

In memory of Edna May Skeels, died January 19, 1895, aged twenty years, six months and fifteen days.

Another star of hope
 is gone,
Another home is dark
 to-day;
Another spirit passing on
 To Heaven's bright,
 celestial way.

This star (a mem'ry loved and cherished so)
Upon the day all patriots love to know,
Its sparkling gleam began—its afterglow
Has brightened time since twenty years ago.

    A mother's love, a mother's tears,
    A mother's care a score of years
    Guided her steps of life aright
    And made for home a shining light.
    The joy of mother, of father, brother,
    And life-time hope of yet another.

When there goes out a star like this one bright
Which 'round the home has shed a radiant light,
We wonder not that darkness spreads its pall.
And throws a shadow o'er the hopes of all.

    The only solace left behind,
        To soothe and heal those broken ties,
    Are farewell words, so sweet, so kind;
        To meet and greet beyond the skies.

CROWNED BY ANGEL HANDS.

[To the memory of Frances E. Willard.]

The world was her field, and human good
Was the broad plain on which she stood,
Battling with mind, and heart, and hand,
"For God and Home and Every Land."
Serenely with ties of love that bind,
She built the hopes of womankind.

   She is gone! And her going,
   To the cultured and knowing,
   Is a sad forsaking,
   And much like the breaking
     Of a branch from the tree,
   Or the out-going of some bright star
   Set as a sentinel in skies afar
     To light, and brighten the home of the free.

   Gone! The wide world is mourning,
   And a nation is frowning
     At the sorrow that is strewn wide and far
   As the act of some demon
   Who would rob us as freemen
     By despoiling the flag of a star.

   Gone! And the moan of the breeze,
   As it sighs through the trees,
     Sings the sad story
   Of the broken-hearted,
   For a loved one departed
     From scenes of her earthly glory,
   To glittering shores where angels throng,
   In worlds of light, and love, and song.

"From Greenland's icy mountains
 From India's coral strand,"
From every state and country
 Of near and distant land,
And e'en from the islands of the seas.
Her praise is born on every breeze
In every clime, by every christian tongue,
The anthems of that praise are sung.

Of life she chose the better part,
And scorned the mockery of art:
From the home of the lowly this woman came
To be crowned with the laurels of a well-earned fame:
As gentle and sweet as the flowers that bloom,
As rich in reverence as the tears at her tomb.
This uncrowned queen of many lands
Has received her crown from angel hands

 Gone from the homes
 Of our land, and from the domes
  Of the churches and temples are ringing
 Those requiem bells
 Whose deep tone tells
 Of the sad deprivation
 That's befallen the nation
  But the angels are joyfully singing.

 Gone! And the grief of the hours,
 And the strewing of flowers,
  And the flow of sad tears,
 Are invoking a tribute of love,
 And sending their message above,
  To honor her labor of years.

Poems of Patriotism.

AN INQUIRY.

Dear "Old Vet" of the fast fading past
Ye who gallantly fought from first to last
Do you suppose the time will come again,
When valiant armies of valiant men,
Will march responsive to their country's call
And fight when fight most likely means to fall?

THE ANSWER.

Ah, friend, I fear the time has not yet come,
When armies treading to the beat of drum
Shall cease to meet, and in fierce war's array,
Assail each other, mangle, wound and slay;
The time will come, however, I believe,
When mankind, learning wisdom, will achieve
Each other's happiness and highest good
By deeds of love and not by deeds of blood;
Then strife will be unknown and war will cease
And all mankind will dwell in love and peace.

—M. H. P.

A "WAH" PROPHECY.

Shud Uncle Sam find out
  Dem Spanyerds sunk de Maine,
    An' blew dem sailors in de sea,
A great big wah wud shuah kum 'bout—
  Like cullud men in Linkum's reign,
    Dem Cubans wud be free.

If wah should ebber kum
  'Twix Uncle Sam and Spain,
    Dem Cubans shuah be free;
We'd heah de beatin' drum
  In de Yankee's army train
    "From Atlanter to de sea."

WEYLER WITH HER YET.

However much old Spain may now abhor
  Her prospects with Insurgent bands
One thing she may be thankful for,
  She still has Weyler on her hands.

WILD NOTES OF WAR.

[During the Venezuela affair.]

Old Jonny Bull has been quite badly scored
By the pen that's mightier than the sword:
There's a war of words a ragin' just now
That may yet result in a world-wide row:
The old vet's blood is boilin' up ag'in.
There's a sight o' talk 'bout musterin' in.

Unless the Old Lion his aggression relaxes.
The Modern Woodmen will whet up their axes
An' saddle the goats on next meetin' night
An' march as cavalry into the fight:
And the K. of P. with helmets flashing
Will show them the art of sabre-slashing.

Uncle Bill Williams who lately came back
From hot pursuit of a wild bear's track.
Way down in the woods of Arkansaw
Where they pay no 'tention to huntin' law.
Has his patriot blood risin' up in him
And is organizin' in battle trim.

He expects to command the volunteers
And make 'em all colonels and brigadiers:
And being familiar with bills of fare
He'll treat the foragin' part with care:
And as a "war measure" to set things aglow.
He's promisin' pensions before they go.

GOING.

Some are going off to war,
   To sail a Cuban sea
   And help make Cuba free
And some not going quite so far,
   For some there be who'd "rarther"
   Go just so far and go no farther.

Some are going with flag and banner,
   Some going now and some next fall,
   And some, perhaps, not going at all.
Some are going to join Camp Tanner,
   Then going not to leave 'er
   "For fear of yellow fever."

Some are off to Klondyke, knowing
   The perils of its cold,
   A-going there for gold.
There's a sight o' talk of "going,"
   Some for glory and some for pay,
And those not going, are going-to stay.

APPROPRIATE EVERYWHERE.

The American Flag is an "all-'round" rag
That floats in victory or waves in peace,
Unfurls in war and when wars cease;
Emblem of country that patriots love,
Its stars are types of those above,
Its glowing colors of red, white and blue,
Mingle together in gorgeous hue;
Its silken folds so rich and sweet
Never appear so pretty and neat,
Are never so graceful as when wars cease,
And it proudly waves as a standard of peace.

POSSIBILITIES.

It wouldn't s'prise me that now purty soon
They'd be singin' songs without any tune,
And some new rule, or some new law,
Beatin' anything the world ever saw,
Would be figured out 'fore very long,
To prove the earth's been revolvin' wrong.

When somethin' else's wanted, all new-fangled,
S'pose they'll fix up the old star-spangled
Banner that floats o'er the land of the free,
In some new rig that'll puzzle you and me
To tell it's our flag—the world and its ways
Hev all changed so since old-time days.

TO HEROES OF THE SEA.

O sing the praise of the jolly tar
   Who braves the dangers of the sea,
Who carries the flag to ports afar,
   O sing it long and joyfully.

O sing of Dewey at Manila bay,
   And let all join the glad refrain,
For daring deeds the first of May
   That sank the ships of treacherous Spain.

O sing of sailors far away,
   Among the perils of a simoon sea,
Of the gallant crews who fought that day
   For the glorious cause of liberty.

O sing of Sampson and Sigsbee and Schley,
   In sun-kissed waters of sultry seas,
Remember the motto that floats mast-high
   Majestic in each passing breeze.

O sing of heroes in time gone by,
   O sing of the heroes of today,
And honor the memory of those who lie
   Beneath the waters of Havana bay.

ODE TO CUBA'S FREEDOM.

O, "Gem of the Antilles" set out in the sea,
Have faith in thy fight for sweet liberty!
An army and navy will rescue thee,
And patriot sons will soon set free,
    Thy fettered band,
      On slave-cursed land!

Free from the hellish tyrant's reign!
Free from the streams of blood that stain
Thy country! Free from fetters of the despot's chain!
Free from the yoke of merciless Spain!
    Free, oh Cuban land,
      From the tyrant's hand!

Fight on, oh Cuban! Americans boast
That patriots thrive along her coast!
Oh fearful thy fate should freedom be lost!
Fight till you vanquish that Spanish host,
    And the tyrants flee
      O'er the trackless sea!

Fight on, oh Cuban! though plantations be curled
In smoke and flame, till the demon is hurled
To sea! On rampart and field let thy flag be unfurled
Till victory is echoed around the world!
    Oh patriot, fight on
      Till thy freedom is won!

The country that gave to liberty birth,
And nurtured its life when there was a dearth
Of sympathy for freedom's glorious worth,
Will aid thee join the republics of earth—
    Thou struggling band
    On Spain-cursed land!

Thy battle, oh Cuba, 'tis not all in vain!
The friends of liberty will never disdain
Thy efforts to sever from Spanish domain,
And the priceless boon of freedom to gain!
    'Tis our message to thee,
    Oh Isle of the sea!

Then let grand monuments upon thy battle plain,
Rise sacred to the memory of thy noble slain
Who resisted the rule of tyrannical Spain,
And sundered the links of the despot's chain—
    When thou'rt set free,
    Oh Gem of the Sea!

TO A BRIDE.

Incomparable thou, oh happy bride,
And yet we would liken the glow of thy pride,
And the lamp of thy love that is burning so bright,
To something of earth or heavenly light:
To laughing waters which down the mountain flow,
Or the lily that blooms in the valley below:
We would liken thy life, thy hope and thy love
To the trusting innocence of a gentle dove,
To the chimes of music or rythm of words,
To the gladsome notes of mating birds
Singing their merriest and sweetest tune:
To the fairest and rarest rose of June
We would liken thee through life to come,
Thou queen of a new and happy home.

TEN LINES TO TEN YEARS.

X

[December 27, 1897.]

Ten years in union have been passed,
The first for love, for love the last:
Ten winters of gay and joyous chime,
Ten summers of flowers and song and rime,
Ten cycles complete of earthly clime,
Ten shadows on the dial of time:
Ten years 'twould take of care and thought,
To tell the things which that ten brought
The toil and trials of that dear ten,
The hopes that fell and rose again.

A MEMORY.

That happy day, one week ago,
   That placed a peaceful crown of light
Upon my life, did well its part
   If one was given you as bright.

A BIRTH-DAY WISH.

Dear friend, I wish for you tonight,
   One hundred years of happy life,
All filled with peace and joyous light,
   All free from danger and from strife.

If every friend should wish for thee,
   As much before tomorrow dawned,
Unending years would be your lot,
   'Twould rob you of your home beyond.

THREE MONTHS OF CHILDHOOD.

This day must picture beauty rare;
It brings event to you quite fair,
And one to us that's ever dear —
It marks three months of thy first year.

CLUBS.

I've heard of clubs since I was born
Until the thought of clubs I fairly scorn:
They're thick as snow-flakes or April showers,
Yes, clubs are trumps in this town of ours.

The boys and girls and women and their hubs
Spend half their time attending clubs:
And all you hear when on the streets
Is something about when the next club meets.

TO A GRADUATING CLASS.

[June 19, 1891.]

You gathered sweet flowers to deck the halls,
And garlands beautiful arrayed the walls:
Mottoes festooned with appropriate wreaths
And "Gang Warily" twined in evergreen leaves.

Your school days are over, before you is life,
With its storm and sunshine, pleasure and strife:
May your pathway ever be strewn with flowers
Which only bloom brighter because of the showers.

GO GATHER THE GEMS.

Go gather the gems from the world's wide field,
  The lights of life, with the darkness dispelled,
And set those stars on one bright shield,
  The likes of whose beauty none ever beheld.

POETIC "FEET" DISPLACED.

The kind o' poems I allus like
   Aint simply those jes' trim an' neat,
Which glide along smooth as yer bike,
   With rime an' rythm all complete,
But words sublime, of deep intent,
   Which sift the chaff out of the wheat
Which form the poem's sentiment
   And kind-a sweep it off its "feet."

A SEVERE STROKE.

'Neath one fell blow our hopes expired,
Ruthlessly crushed by the girl that's hired,
Perusing the columns of the dear old TIMES,
Her optics caught onto one of our rimes
She read it through and with earnest face,
Reflecting the honesty of her race,
Glanced at her mistress with an inquiring look
Asking the question: "Hez yer husband a book"
(Oh, shades of chagrin! "A book!" "A book!")
"From which this poem was 'riginally took?"

SUSPICIOUS OF THE BRITISH.

'Tis said the most apparent reason why
   That this world's brightly beaming sun
Ne'er leaves its orbit in the sky,
   Nor feels its task but just begun,
And never sits on England's vast domain,
   Because the Lord so fears the British shark,
And knows so well his greed for gold and gain,
   He will not trust him in the dark.

DREAM OF THE TEACHER MAN.

One calm and still November night,
    The teacher man
Dreamed a dream of great delight;
    A prize-trip plan
Lay pictured out before his mind,
    And many a scheme
Kindred to wishes of his kind,
    Was solved by dream.

Just how secure the votes to win
    That glorious prize—
A thing that ever puzzled him
    With opened eyes—
All seemed clear in rapturous dreams;
    And midst this spell
Nature's grandest view, where beauty teems,
    Across his vision fell.

And then this dreamy teacher man,
    Of whom we tell—
Who thought he'd found a winning plan
    Awakened from his spell.
How disappointing it must have been
    To one like him involved,
E'en though by dream in earnest hope to win,
    To have that hope dissolved!

WAYS OF THE WORLD.

Of all the people to church who go,
    This day and age, the number is few
    Who seek a seat in a forward pew;
But let it be to an opera show,
    For an evening of the world's to-do,
    It may be said, alas how true!
They take their seat in "bald-head row."

THE WRITER AND THE FIGHTER.

An author and a pugilist met one day,
The writer grave, the fighter gay,
And as the two did wander along,
So goes the story and the song.
This was what they were heard to say:
(The author grave and the fighter gay)
"Oh what shall I write today?"
"Oh whom shall I fight today?"
And the writer wrote and wrote and thought,
And the fighter fought and fought and fought.
One with his pen which he dips and shoves,
The other equipped with lips and gloves.
The writer's writings came to naught
And the fighter got whipped in the fight he fought.
The author no longer in the ink doth plunge
And the fighter has quit and thrown up the sponge.

REGULATED BY THE MOON.

Don't blame the boys who go to Crescent for a "smile,"
  Or down at Old Town to practice many a "shine,"
When the old moon sets and example vile,
  And in a single month gets "full" a second time.

EDITORS TAKE IT TOO.

That measly old monster
  Surnamed "La Grippe,"
Who is takin' in America
  On a two years' trip,
Invaded our sanctum
  By an infamous sneak
And caught the editor
  In his "grip" this week.

TRIUMPH.

Oft-times the ordeals of misfortune dire,
   Survived, resisted, o'erpowered and outdone,
Impel us on with new fervor and zeal,
   And life is more glorious for battles won.

LIFE LINES.

A "Life Line" held by friendly hands
May rescue one from sinking sands,
Or guide them from some danger shore,
Where clouds are gathering more and more,
To hope's inland, where sun-bright rays
Dispel the mists of dismal ways
Where life's ambition is recast
And freed from turmoil of a past.

www.ingramcontent.com/pod-product-compliance
Lightning Source LLC
Chambersburg PA
CBHW021936160426
43195CB00011B/1116